A long-haired satin cinnamon hamster. Photo by M. Gilroy.

Hamsters

Edited and Revised by Dr. G. Edgar Folk, Jr., Department of Physiology, College of Medicine, State University of Iowa

Acknowledgments

This guide to the proper care and raising of hamsters is based on the booklet, "Hamsters for Pleasure and Profit" by J. M. Graber, with added material from articles that originally appeared in All-Pets Magazine. *Included among these are: "General Notes on Golden Hamsters," "Buying Your First Hamster," "Handling Hamsters," "Housing Hamsters," Jean E. Cook, F.Z.S.; "Housing and Equipment," H. W. Reynolds; "Importance of Milk," Leonore Brandt; "Hamsters in Medical Science," Dr. Banner Bill Morgan; "Care of Pet Hamsters," Ernest P. Walker. The chapter on Breeding Exhibition Hamsters was contributed by H. Deaton and T. W. Pond.*

Second Edition, Revised

Distributed in the UNITED STATES by T.F.H. Publications, Inc., 211 West Sylvania Avenue, Neptune City, NJ 07753; in CANADA by H & L Pet Supplies Inc., 27 Kingston Crescent, Kitchener, Ontario N2B 2T6; Rolf C. Hagen Ltd., 3225 Sartelon Street, Montreal 382 Quebec; in ENGLAND by T.F.H. Publications Limited, 4 Kier Park, Ascot, Berkshire SL5 7DS; in AUSTRALIA AND THE SOUTH PACIFIC by T.F.H. (Australia) Pty. Ltd., Box 149, Brookvale 2100 N.S.W., Australia; in NEW ZEALAND by Ross Haines & Son, Ltd., 18 Monmouth Street, Grey Lynn, Auckland 2 New Zealand; in SINGAPORE AND MALAYSIA by MPH Distributors Pte., 71-77 Stamford Road, Singapore 0617; in the PHILIPPINES by Bio-Research, 5 Lippay Street, San Lorenzo Village, Makati Rizal; in SOUTH AFRICA by Multipet Pty. Ltd., 30 Turners Avenue, Durban 4001. Published by T.F.H. Publications Inc., Ltd. the British Crown Colony of Hong Kong.

Contents

All photos by M. Gilroy

Cover photo: Cream hamster by M. Gilroy.

Hamsters make amazing pets. They are soft and cuddly and very entertaining for children. Your local petshop will have suitable cages and games from which you can choose.

Origin and Characteristics

In 1930, Mr. I. Aharoni, a professor of the Department of Zoology, Hebrew University, Jerusalem, decided to explore an animal burrow near Aleppo, Syria. At the end of an eight-foot tunnel he came upon a mother with her twelve young—the first Golden Hamsters to be found alive in nearly a century. This rare species was known as *Mesocricetus auratus*. Professor Aharoni took his find back to Hebrew University. Some of the young died during the journey and some after their arrival. Finally, only one male and two females survived. Four months later, one of the two females gave birth to a litter, the first to be born in captivity.

In 1931, two pairs of descendants of these hamsters were sent to England where they were found to be valuable laboratory animals. In 1938, Golden Hamsters arrived for the first time in the United States at the Public Health Service in Carville, Louisiana. It is estimated that in this country alone in 1950, the level-off point of their popularity, they numbered 100,000, all of them descended from the family that Professor Aharoni discovered near Aleppo.

Hamsters are very popular pets because they are inexpensive, hardy, tame and come in many colors and coats. All the domesticated hamsters in the world today originated from two pairs found in Syria.

Origin and Characteristics

Characteristics

Exactly what is this creature which attained so much popularity in so few years? The Golden Hamster is a small rodent, measuring, in a good specimen, about six to seven inches and weighing, when fully adult, three to four and a half ounces. It resembles a miniature bear, with fur that is dense and sleek, of a deep, rich gold, carrying an undercoat which ranges from medium to dark gray, according to the shade of the top coat. The belly fur, although originally light gray, is becoming very much whiter in present-day hamsters, while the head, once narrow and ratlike, is growing shorter through selective breeding. The cheeks carry bands or flashes; and a dark, broad band of fur runs, sometimes completely unbroken, across the chest. The tail, short and stumpy, is approximately one-third to one-half inch long; the large ears are set well apart; healthy eyes are bright and bold, expressing a lively curiosity, which seems to be characteristic of this fascinating animal.

On each side of its face, extending from the cheek back to the shoulder, the hamster is supplied with an unbelievably elastic pouch that is not connected with the digestive organs. The skin is so extremely loose and pliable that the animal can be lifted or held by a fold of the skin. The front feet are somewhat like hands. The rear legs and feet have three functions: They carry the hamster on all-fours, support his weight in a sitting position, and enable him to move backward. The third function is useful in the native habitat when the hamster needs to retreat into his burrow.

Hamsters make great pets.

Origin and Characteristics

Three Species of Hamsters

Speaking of native habitat, it is interesting to know something about the hamster's history, geographical distribution, and habits. The animal that has been abundant in Europe for many years is the common Giant Hamster, which is from eight to twelve inches long. This species is fierce, untamable, and unsatisfactory for laboratory use, as is also the Dwarf Hamster, *Cricetulus* (two and one-half to four inches long). The

Our pet hamster from Syria is in the middle as far as size is concerned in the three hamsters now known to science. The Giant Hamster reaches one foot in length and is found in Germany. The Dwarf Chinese Hamster, from Asia, reaches a maximum of four inches.

Habits of Hamsters

Giant Hamster is most abundantly found in Germany, near Thuringen, Saxony, and all along the Rhine River. From the German word *hamstern,* meaning to store or hoard, comes the name we know. And when one realizes that from sixty to a hundred pounds of grain have been found in the burrows of the Giant Hamster, the name seems admirably chosen. Little wonder that wild hamsters are regarded as destructive pests by European farmers.

The hamster which is today in such widespread use in the United States and with which this book is concerned is *Mesocricetus auratus,* genus *Mesocricetus,* species *auratus,* or, simply, the Syrian Golden Hamster.

In their native state Golden Hamsters inhabit waste and pasture lands and grain fields. They are capable of burrowing from one and a half to eight feet to nest. Up to this time the Golden Hamster has been located only in Asia Minor. In the wild state, if food and water become scarce while the mother is still nursing her litter, she may become highly carnivorous, preying on the nests of birds, mice, and other small animals to supply the food and drink she and her young need. Generally, however, grains are the staple diet.

General Habits

Unquestionably, one of the most attractive features of the hamster, one which has made it a valued pet, is a complete lack of odor and a general cleanliness. Moreover, domesticated hamsters are naturally

Hamsters are great pets. They eat almost anything that isn't poisonous to humans, especially grains, fruits and vegetables. They are clean and have no odor.

Habits of Hamsters

tame, requiring only a short training period to make them charming pets. Especially friendly are grown males and unbred females, although, generally, males make the best pets. Primarily, hamsters are nocturnal animals, reserving the night for their social life. Measurements with cages set on springs show that unless disturbed these animals

Males make the best pets, though virgin females are almost as tame.

perform over ninety percent of their total activity when their cages are in darkness. Nevertheless, they are easily aroused and ready for play any time their attention is attracted.

The two best-known and most-often-recalled characteristics of the hamster are its hoarding habits and its short gestation period. The pouches on either side of the face can hold up to half the animal's weight in food. The hamster delights in taking food, filling its pouches, and scurrying off to a corner of the cage, where it can disgorge the contents and leisurely eat the hoarded food. In fact, a well-stocked food pile is important to a hamster's sense of well-being. It is a wise owner who, in spite of his desire to keep the cage clean, does not often disturb the hoarded treasure.

Gestation Period

The gestation period is sixteen days for the average hamster, although a young doe may go for as long as eighteen days. The litter may number anywhere from two to fifteen. The young leave the mother after three to four weeks; then, after a rest of three or four days, she is ready to breed again. Since hamsters reach mature breeding age at two or three months, their short gestation period—the shortest of any mammal—and the short periods between litters make them extremely prolific.

Habits of Hamsters

To illustrate this extraordinary fecundity, let us assume that you have purchased a pair of hamsters of breeding age and that you breed them on January 1 and every time thereafter, giving the female time to wean her young and to have proper rest. By July 1, she will have given birth to thirty or more young, more than sixty-five percent of which are females. By July 1, she will be grandmother to 431, making a total of 543 from just one female in six months, estimating six to a litter.

Don't allow your hamster the freedom of your house no matter how tame he appears. They investigate everything and since they have no fears, a rat or cat can easily catch them.

Other Interesting Characteristics

As just described, fairly well-known hamster characteristics are the large cheek pouches, the short tail, the gentle but inquisitive nature, the complete absence of odor, and the sixteen-day gestation period. Other characteristics of hamsters, not so well known are that

a. they hibernate in cold weather;
b. they sometimes semi-hibernate (estivate) in warm weather; and
c. they have an unusually low normal body temperature.

These three characteristics must somehow interrelate. Some dealers, ignorant of this peculiar temperature-regulation of hamsters, have thrown valuable animals out for dead, only to find later that they had merely taken a normal course to a frigid vacation by sinking into a cold sleep, called hibernation. This state may occur with about one-third of a colony of hamsters if they are forced to live in a temperature of 40° to 50° F. Of course, if they stay in a warm nest, they will not feel the cold outside air. Normally, their body temperature is like that of man. With experience one can place a human mouth-thermometer in the cheek pouch or the colon of

Purchasing Your Initial Stock

the hamster. The reading will be about 99° F, an unusually low temperature compared, for example, to that of white rats—102° F. In hibernation, the stiffened body of the hamster drops to a temperature close to that of the cold air surrounding it, and the heart rate and the breathing rate become about five a minute. It takes from thirty to sixty minutes for the hamster to wake up from hibernation.

Semi-hibernation, or estivation, has been frequently observed, even when the cage temperature is somewhere between 70 and 80° F. It has been erroneously called "sleepers' disease." It is harmless and occurs normally also in chipmunks, ground squirrels, and prairie dogs. It can be recognized by the effects of disturbing the animal: At first, it is lifeless and stiff; then it will tremble in all four limbs. In about five minutes it will be running around in the cage in completely normal fashion.

Golden Hamsters are fascinating as well as useful animals. It is little wonder that as the demand for them increases, more and more people become interested in raising them commercially. Their prolificness, gentle temperament, lack of odor, and the ease and economy of caring for them make hamster-raising an inviting occupation.

When beginning to raise hamsters, the most important step is the purchase of stock, since at that time ignorance may spell early discouragement to the commercial breeder or to the fancier. You simply cannot expect to get good offspring from poor parents. In securing satisfactory breeding stock, you need not pay exorbitant prices, but you very much need to know what to look for.

First of all, don't look for bargains—culls or laboratory-test survivors—but buy hamsters which are sold for breeding stock. Depending on age, good males and females ready for breeding should weigh from three to four ounces. Pre-breeders are about the size of the palm of your hand, breeders a little longer. To reproduce well, both the male and the female should be fairly calm, although a female that does not want the male in the pen with her may make a good mother. Never choose your hamster from a cage containing both sexes of all ages, else you may find yourself with an unwanted family bred from a much-too-young female.

What are the essentials to look for in appearance? Principally, look for all-round signs of health: soft, silken fur; bright, prominent eyes; and a general solidity of body. Never buy a bony hamster. Next, scrutinize the

Housing and Maintenance

ears, which are a good indication of the hamster's breeding span. In a young hamster, the inside ear is covered with white hairs, which gradually disappear with age. Never buy a hamster with naked, shiny ears—an indication that he is past his prime. Occasionally, hamsters with nicked ears are sold as breeders. This trait does not detract from their value (although perhaps slightly from their appearance), since it is simply a means of identifying members of a certain herd.

Having determined the age of the hamster, look once again at its ears, but this time also look at the nose, feet, and belly. Never choose an animal showing the faintest trace of pimples in these areas. The pimples may be the beginning of mange and mean endless work for you. There is no guaranteed cure for this highly infectious disease.

The price of breeding stock will, of course, vary with its location and its quality. Choose a reputable source, and you will receive a fair price for the quality of hamster that you raise.

The two principal considerations for housing your hamsters are their comfort and their safety. Light, air, and sufficient space for exercise are necessities. Dark, dreary hutches reeking of creosote, in which an animal languished or slept from one meal to the next, are wholly unsuitable.

In constructing or purchasing cages, one should remember that the hamster is especially fond of gnawing. For this reason, knotty or cracked lumber, or flimsy boards are unsuitable. Metal cages are sometimes objected to because of the condensation of moisture on them. Asbestos shingles are excellent building materials and may be used in place of wood. However, the following instructions are all given in terms of metal, wood, and hardware cloth, or wire. When wood is used, even though it is hard and the construction sound, the cages should be inspected occasionally to make sure that gnawing has not damaged them severely.

Pens for Hamsters

Designs for pens are many and varied—from the simple housing for one pet to the elaborate

12

Housing and Maintenance

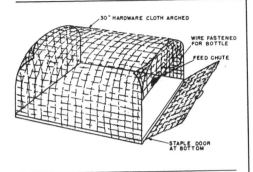

It's cheaper and better to buy a hamster cage at your local pet dealer, but for emergencies you can construct a cage as shown above.

arrangements of a commercial breeder. Of course, your pet shop carries many cages designed especially to be used to house hamsters. These cages are convenient to use, economical to purchase, and available in different designs. If, however, you'd like to try your hand at making a cage, we include here samples of the simplest and the more complex designs. Instructions for making the various cages are given first and then for outfitting them, since the same things may be used in any size or type of pen.

For the single pet, allowing for an area of *at least* one square foot, a simple cage can be made from two deep baking pans, either round or square, and hardware cloth or wire. Adult hamsters can crawl through spaces the size of a quarter, and

babies through openings less than one-half inch. For a breeding cage, one-quarter- or one-third-inch hardware cloth is most suitable. The wire mesh is shaped into a cylinder or square (depending on the pans), about ten inches high. Where the wire mesh meets, plenty of overlap should be allowed. This is set into one pan, and the other pan is put on top of it. While extremely easy to build and to maintain, such a cage is also durable enough for a pet hamster, gnawproof, and convenient to clean.

More serious breeders can make a small breeding set-up as shown below. Hamsters like the dark. In nature they live in deep tunnels.

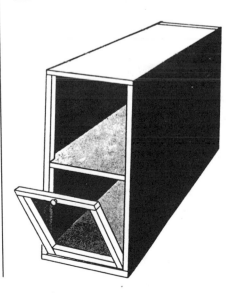

13

Housing and Maintenance

A Cage Made from a Fruit Box

Another cage that is economical and suited to the beginner can be made from a fruit box. Go to your nearest market and ask for a one-by-two-foot box with a solid center compartment. Take it apart and you have three one-by-one-foot pieces, slightly over one-half inch thick. These will be just right; the two-foot sides are too thin. From the three solid pieces you may cut the strips for your frame. Take one piece and rule down a strip an inch wide on one side; mark off another strip just like that on the second piece; then saw them off. On the third piece, remove the first strip one inch wide and then mark down another on the same side and cut it off. The third piece is now an inch narrower than the first two. The first two pieces are placed parallel and the third piece inserted between them and nailed in place, so that you now have the top, bottom, and one end of the cage. Next, you need hardware cloth or an old window ventilating screen (the kind that pulls apart). Fasten this to the wood to form the two sides of the box. Place supports on either side of the open end of the cage around which the wire may be stapled.

Now you are ready to make your door. Use the four strips cut from the original sides of the fruit box for the frame, trimming them to size (they must be inserted between the top and bottom of the cage). Wire the frame from the inside of the door to protect the wood, but be sure that the screening does not overlap, else the door will stick. You can insert your door to swing open sideways, or you can let it swing downward to open. If you choose the latter, the chances of the animal dropping out are almost eliminated. You may fasten the door to the cage by means of small hinges. However, two nails driven through the supports and door on opposite sides, about three-quarters of an inch from the bottom, directly in the center of the pieces, will serve as well.

The Oldfield Pen

One of the cages best adapted for keeping hamsters—any number—is the Oldfield Pen, designed by a member of the British Hamster Club. It has easy access, is simple to clean, and can be constructed by anyone who has a vise.

Basically, it consists of a simple box of *hard* wood, three-eighths of an inch to one-half inch thick,

Housing and Maintenance

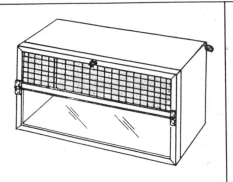

The Oldfield pen is still one which is favored because of its simplicity of design and the fact that it can almost be made entirely of scrap materials.

These will later have to be removed to be riveted to the door frame. A strip of angle fitted to the bottom edge holds the glass and prevents the bedding material from escaping.

Fit the door frame to the two angle pieces (which hold the glass) with two small strap-hinges; the rivets which hold these hinges hold also the bottom corners of the door frame. Fix this to the pen.

Fasten the door with a cabinet spring catch, one part riveted to the

But for ease of care and cleanliness, a factory-made hamster cage, available from almost every petshop, is the best.

approximately twenty-four inches long, twelve inches high, and twelve inches wide. The entire front of the pen is made from aluminum angle three-quarters inch by three-quarters inch by one-sixteenth inch thick, the lower half holding the glass window, the upper half of one-half-inch mesh wire netting being framed in the same angle, which has been closed up in a vise.

Cut the angle to size for the door frame (which opens outward and downward), making sure that the top half is slightly less than the bottom half. Clamp closely, with the netting between, in a vise; and rivet each top corner.

Fit a piece of angle to each lower side of the box, leaving sufficient space for the glass to slide between.

Housing and Maintenance

top center of the door and the other secured by two screws just inside the pen.

Paint the whole of the inside with a non-toxic paint, and the outside as you wish. One thing must be emphasized: The gap between the glass is intentional; a one-quarter-inch gap should be left in order to prevent the hamster's feet from being trapped when the door is opened or closed.

A Breeding Cage

The following instructions are for a breeding cage suitable for large- or small-scale operations. These cages can be stacked on top of one another, alongside each other, or back to back to form aisles. Each cage is a double unit—one compartment on top and one at the bottom. It is constructed of twelve-inch lumber. You will need one-quarter-inch hardware cloth two feet wide, twelve-inch lumber, a few box nails, and some staples. From the twelve-inch lumber, cut off two feet; next, cut off three fifteen-inch pieces. Nail two of these on either end of the two-foot length. The third one is the center shelf. Nail these in place; stand the frame upright on one of the fifteen-inch sides, and you have something that looks like a capital "E."

A real treat for your hamster is a plastic globe. The hamster gets inside and runs for hours . . . doing up to 4 miles a day!

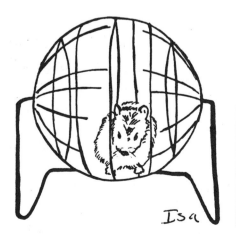

Captions
A long-haired hamster, p. 17; a light chocolate hamster in a ferris wheel, p. 18; a long-haired satin chocolate roan male, top p. 19; a light gray tortoiseshell hamster, bottom p. 19; neither hamsters nor parakeets should be allowed to roam freely in the house, top p. 20; handling the hamster by the scruff of the neck demonstrates the sexual characteristics of this male very clearly, bottom p. 20; a light cream hamster and a red-eyed white hamster, top p. 21; a cream mother with her 11 day old litter, p. 21; a black-eyed white (compare to red-eyed white on p. 21) p. 22; baby hamsters 30 minutes old, top p. 23; 12 days old, bottom p. 23; a normal hamster with its cheek pouches stuffed, p. 24.
All photos by M. Gilroy.

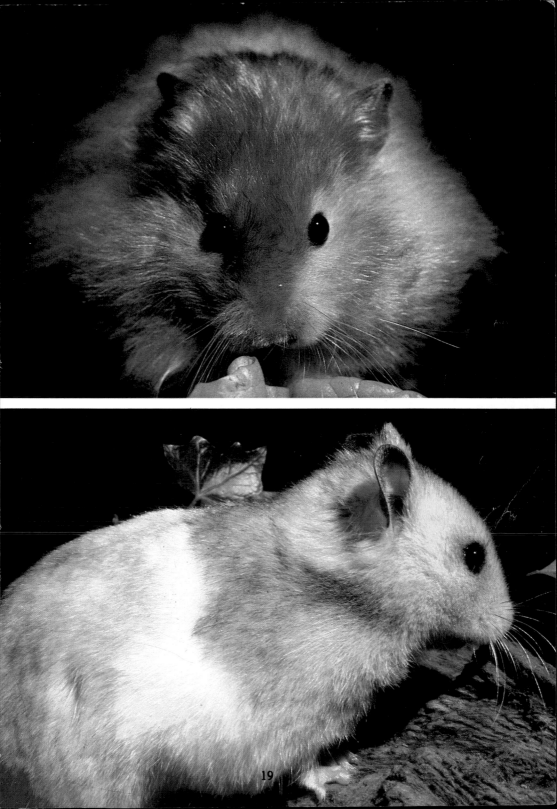

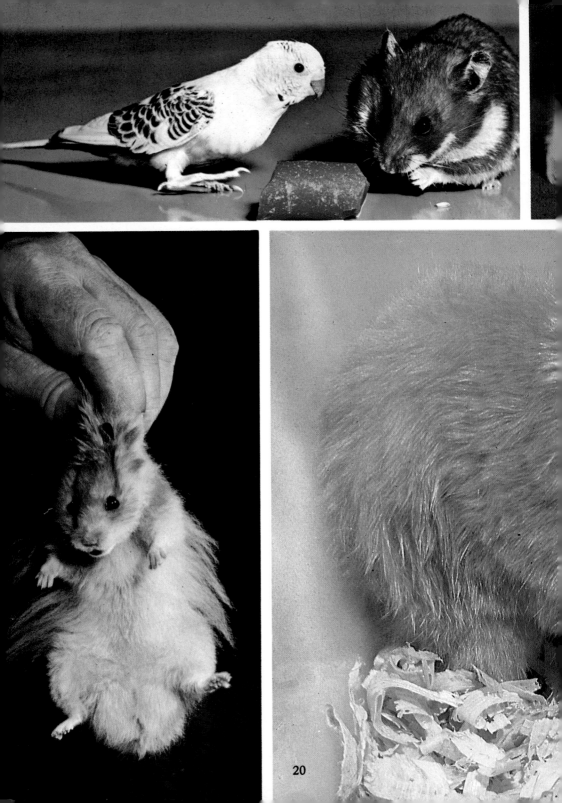

Housing and Maintenance

Now lay the "E" on its side and cut strips for pillars to hold your cage in shape at the end where the door will be, making these the same length as the space between the floor and ceiling. After placing these, cut off fifteen inches of two-foot wire and staple it on the sides, fastening it over the pillars or supports. Now, you must make your door frames—very simply with a frame of lumber covered with wire. Cut the frames a little smaller than the opening into which they will fit, or plane off the inside of the top frame and the outside of the lower frame. They can be fixed to swing open, as we described when discussing the fruit-box cage.

The Breeder-Cage Colony Unit

A companion to the breeding cage is the breeder-cage colony unit. It is built like the regular breeding cage, except that you cut the three pieces twenty-four inches instead of fifteen inches long. This gives each compartment one-by-two-foot floor space, large enough to house twenty-four young at weaning time. The males are put in one compartment, the females in the other.

A Recreation Pen

The last cage may be termed a recreation pen, although it can serve

Every cage must be safe against an attack by a cat or rat.

as an attractive show cage, especially the arched type. If you want to stack these cages, you can make them square. One piece of twelve-inch by fifteen-inch lumber and one piece of hardware cloth twenty-four to thirty inches long, depending on the desired height, are the only materials required.

Cut off a piece of wire the same length as the desired height and the same width as the floorboard. Staple this to the back of the cage floor and join the sides of the arch with wire or pig rings; bend the upper corners and fasten. Don't leave any large spaces between the fastenings.

The door will fit only two-thirds of the way up one end. Fold the wire double for added strength. Hammer staples in over the wire at the bottom—only halfway to give swinging room. The upper one-third of the door end is actually a little longer than an exact proportion of one-third so that the door when closed overlaps it—an added precaution to prevent the hamster's escape.

Now fasten the door. Take a drinking bottle and fasten it with wire to the upper section; then insert the drinking tube through a hole in the wire of the door. You now have a handsome and easily constructed cage. Put a feed chute

in the upper arch at the front, and you will need to open it very little. Be sure to nail a metal strip about two inches wide all around the bottom of the floorboard after you have wired the cage. If you feed pellets, the hamster will take them to his favorite corner, where the treasured loot will fall through one-half inch wire.

A hamster cage should be easily cleaned and accessible for putting in feed.

Housing and Maintenance

Furnishing a Cage

What about furnishing the interiors? If the cage has a hardware cloth or wire bottom, you need only provide some *soft* hay, wood shavings, or excelsior for bedding. The hamster will arrange these materials to suit his needs. If you choose floors, then dry sawdust, ground corncobs, cane, peanut shells, or any clean, absorbent material is adequate.

There is an excellent reason for having "built-in" feeding facilities for at least part of your cages. If you open and close the cage doors very often during the period the young are with their mother, she may put them in her pouches in order to protect them—and there they will suffocate.

Drinking Bottles and Drinking Dishes

Inexpensive drinking bottles and dishes are available at pet shops; but again, if you'd like to try your hand at making them, such water bottles and dishes are easy to devise.

Any bottle similar to a soft-drink container will serve as a drinking bottle. A close-fitting cork to stop the bottle-opening is drilled to allow the entry of a small, about quarter-inch, glass drinking tube. Copper tubing may be substituted. The tube

Your local petshop probably has a hamster kit which includes a cage, feed, cedar chips, water bottle and just about everything you need!

Housing and Maintenance

is then heated and bent to an angle of forty-five degrees. Its end is placed in an opening into the cage and the bottle is secured to the outside of the cage.

Low drinking dishes can be made by cutting tin cans down to a height of one and one-half inches. Hammer the edge smooth and you have a dish that will not rust, tip, or spill; and the young will not be able to drown in it. By the time the babies can climb up these drinkers, they are also old enough to climb out, should they fall in. Some breeders use sardine-can drinking dishes for a mother and her young. However, hamsters are inclined to use them for bathing. Although this may be a good way to housebreak the animals, these dishes require extra cleaning to avoid contamination.

Feeding Chutes

To continue with the "built-in" features, a feeding chute is a very useful facility. A chute opening into the cage simplifies feeding and, as previously discussed, eliminates disturbing mothers with litters. The opening in the cage door, where the chute is placed, should be quite small; otherwise, the young hamsters can crawl through it.

A hamster must chew to keep the front teeth (incisors) from growing too long. It is capable of reducing a piece of wood to shreds without damaging the teeth.

Housing and Maintenance

Your petshop has amazing hamster homes . . . many can be enlarged with special houses, baths and tunnels . . . making them as large as you want.

There is no need to provide interior food containers. Hamsters, hoarding by instinct, will carry off the food to their chosen corners for leisurely consumption. Occasionally, a hamster will choose the water dish as its miser's den. However, there is no point in trying to re-educate it; simply provide another water dish.

Aquariums and terrariums make excellent hamster cages.

As hamsters have been inbred and inbred for a hundred generations or more, only the tamest animals, those most adaptable to domestication, are successful. Thus even a normal cage can be used for breeding. It helps, though, to cover three sides of the cage with cardboard to keep down the light and shield the breeder from noise and strange movements.

An all-glass aquarium is probably the best hamster set-up for commercial breeders since most petshops sell "leakers" very inexpensively, and the hamster doesn't care if the tank leaks or not . . . and neither should you. Be sure to get a top for the aquarium!

Housing and Maintenance

Cage Cleaning and Sanitation

To ensure your hamster's health, it is necessary to clean the cage at least once a week. Hamsters themselves have no parasites, and their feces are odorless. In fact, they clean themselves with their front paws in cat-like, semi-circular motions. Thorough cage cleaning, like feeding, must be made an essential part of your *regular* routine. A pancake turner makes a good tool with which to scoop and scrape the cage floor. Perhaps you may not want to wash the cages every week; but for a thorough cleaning hot, soapy water and a stiff brush are best. A mild disinfectant also may be used. Of course, if you have a cage with a wire bottom, through which the droppings can fall, your problem is simplified; but in one corner of the wire floor a hard mass of solidified urine will form. This must be broken off every few weeks and the floor scrubbed with a wire brush.

The floor litter should be removed entirely at each weekly cleaning to be replaced with fresh litter. By not feeding too many greens at one time, there will be no spoilage. Cages of sick hamsters should be completely washed and disinfected before they are used again.

Your petshop should have various toys which provide amusement for both you and your hamster. Don't use regular children's toys since hamsters chew on the plastic and it must be safe in case they swallow some.

Except for the solid corner, a cage containing a mother and her litter should not be thoroughly cleaned until the cubs' eyes have opened. After the young are about sixteen days old—when the eyes open—the cage should be cleaned well and the nesting material removed and renewed. At this time, it is best not to handle the mother; instead, entice her into a can or a jar, as explained under the topic of handling.

The hamstery, no matter where it is located, must be kept free from rodents and predators. When using rodent killer, remember that the

31

Housing and Maintenance

hamsters also can die from the same poison. The hamstery should also be ventilated, especially in summer.

A few suggestions for keeping your hamsters clean and healthy: Observe newly purchased animals in isolation for a few days before putting them with the rest of the herd. Keep visitors away from hamsters as much as possible. Although they are disease-free, they are extremely susceptible to human diseases. Protect them from yourself when you have a cold or other ailment by exercising scrupulous personal cleanliness. In such cases, some breeders advise the wearing of a gauze mask over nose and mouth.

Raising Hamsters Outdoors

Hamsters thrive most satisfactorily in a temperature ranging from 50° to 80° F, but they can adjust to any climate and humidity. During warm

These hamster houses are all interconnected, making them into a real hamster "village."

Housing and Maintenance

If you only want one hamster, your petshop has a small hamster kit, not as complete as the one shown on page 27.

weather, the cages, and the room in which they are kept, must be well ventilated. Food and water must be looked after carefully. Hamsters can also be housed safely outdoors if they are protected from the cold. While adult hamsters can endure freezing temperatures, the young, born naked, should be raised in a sheltered place. In an outdoor hamstery, the cages may be arranged like tiers in a rabbitry, with overhanging roofs to give protection from driving rain, snow, and sleet. During very cold weather, extra provision for ample nesting materials is needful. Scraps of wool or flannel material are welcomed by the nesting female, since they make soft, warm linings. Tissue paper, if used as nesting material, may stick to the hairless young.

Nest boxes made out of any kind of lumber can be used in place of the added bedding. They should be at least six inches square, with an opening in the front at least three inches in diameter. The circular opening should be covered with strips of tin or some other "gnaw-proof" material so that the mother cannot destroy the nest too quickly.

If the hamsters are kept outside in temperatures below freezing, they should have a water dish of heavy china, about as thick and heavy as a cold-cream jar, which freezing water will not crack. Water bottles are not satisfactory, since the ice is difficult to remove from them, and the tubing can withstand very little ice pressure.

Feeding Your Hamster

Hamsters can endure even sub-zero temperatures for short periods without ill effects. However, if the air gets below 50° F, about one-third of your animals may hibernate. Then the non-hibernating animals may eat the hibernators. Also in cold temperatures the female will breed less frequently than in warmer ones.

The proper feeding of hamsters is a vital aspect of producing sound breeders and litters. There is nothing difficult about supplying the feed or inducing hamsters to eat. The breeder's responsibility is to feed at a set time each day rations that are well balanced and not lacking variety.

Some children find hamsters so fascinating they get their friends together and accumulate a large hamster village with innumerable racing wheels, tunnels, etc. Most hamster castles have the potential to add on.

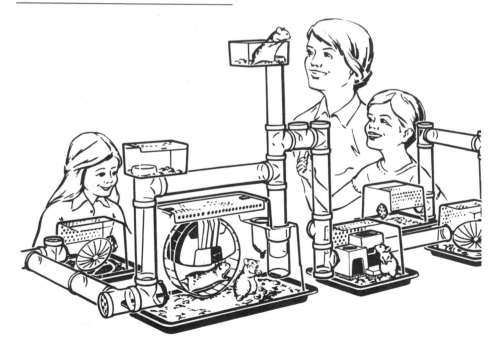

Feeding Your Hamster

A Variety of Foods

Hamsters will eat approximately the same foods a rabbit does, except that they are not very fond of hay. They relish grain of any kind, pellets, and most kinds of fresh fruits and vegetables. Although it is not possible to list all their favored foods here, a sampling can be given to indicate the variety. Desirable proteins are wheat, corn, barley, oats, sunflower seed, soybeans, and many kinds of nuts. A variety of pellets is also acceptable, ranging from dog foods to livestock pellets, as given to rabbits, other fur-bearers, and fowl. The pellets, which must be fresh, should be stored in a tight container in a cool place. Under no condition should any pellet food contain less than twenty percent protein. Scrutinize the list of ingredients printed on the container carefully before you purchase. The kinds of vegetables and fruits hamsters like include the following: lettuce, carrots and tops, watermelon rinds, banana peels, apples, grapes, and all vegetable trimmings discarded daily at your local market. Even grass and dandelions suit the easily pleased hamster. Cabbage should be fed rarely, as animals maintained on cabbage, pellets, and water become poor breeders and suffer from overweight. A practical and convenient method of obtaining green foods for your hamster is to get the greens your grocer discards. He will probably be glad to give them to you, if only you will pick them up regularly. Thus you can establish an economical and dependable year-round source of fresh food.

Petshops have special treats for hamsters. This aids in keeping their chewing teeth in condition. It also keeps them healthy.

Feeding Your Hamster

Garlic and onions are unsuitable, and citrus fruits are considered a poor food for hamsters. A controversial topic is whether or not to feed raw meat. Some fanciers maintain that raw meat should not be fed under any conditions, certainly not to mothers with young, since presumably it encourages cannibalism. Others opine that raw meat has exactly the opposite effect in that it discourages cannibalism, especially in mothers with young! In their primitive stage, hamsters subsist largely on grains; but occasionally they become carnivorous, shown by the number of insects they will eat. It is best to feed raw meat on a trial basis at first. If the results are satisfactory, then such feeding may be continued.

Wheat-Germ Oil and Milk

Two additional important elements in the hamster's diet are wheat-germ oil, containing vitamin E, and milk. Feeding wheat-germ oil tends to maintain continuous good reproduction. It may be dropped onto the bread or rolled oats or else given the hamster from the end of an eyedropper. Vitamin E is particularly important during fall and winter breeding.

Hamster foods can be in seed form or in large chunk, it really doesn't matter.

Although milk, in small quantities, is a valuable addition to any hamster's diet, bred females, nursing mothers, and young litters must have it. In the young, it helps to develop healthy bone structure, thus preventing loss of calcium and ensuring continued productivity in the matron. Some hamster breeders assert that this milk eliminates nursing pain, a condition which causes some nervous females to eat their young. Diluted evaporated milk or fresh pasteurized milk may be offered; *never offer raw milk.*

Feeding Routine

Hamsters are fed once a day. Being creatures of habit, they will soon adjust themselves to whatever time of day you choose to feed

Feeding Your Hamster

them. If you feed them every week-day, and give them a larger portion on Saturday, you may skip the Sunday meal and give yourself a rest. The part-time furrier, whose hamsters are a sideline, can feed half of his herd one day and half the next. Hamsters eat only for their immediate needs. They may, without opening their eyes, reach into the corner for a bite during the day; but being nocturnal, they usually wait until the evening for their main meal. If hamsters find you cleaning out their "pantry" too often, especially when they have hoarded a few choice delicacies, they will go to sleep with their pouches full of food. Avoid giving too much food that might spoil; this includes, for instance, green foods or soybean sprouts. The hamster will regulate his own feeding, if you provide enough variety and quantity. Remember: Plenty of proteins and plenty of greens are essential to their diet.

Hamsters can, if necessary, live without water, provided they are well supplied with greens. However, except for experiments, it is far better to provide a steady supply of fresh, clean water.

When the young are about ten days old but still blind, they will stroll about in search of food. If the mother does not see them and drag them back to the nest, they will continue to look for things like carrot tops and other greens. You may feed them rolled oats at this early age.

As to quantity—a mother with a litter of six, sixteen days old, can be given a small carrot (about three and

Commercially packaged food for small mammals (hamsters, gerbils, guinea pigs, rats, and mice) is nutritionally adequate, inexpensive, convenient, and available in pet stores and supermarkets.

Handling Hamsters

a-half inches long) with greens, and one of the following items: three tablespoonfuls of pellets, two tablespoonfuls of rolled oats, or one slice of stale bread. This is more than they will eat. A hamster will generally drink about two tablespoonfuls of water and eat one tablespoonful of food, either green or dry, daily.

Don't allow your child to overfeed the hamster. Uneaten food sours.

Golden hamsters are tame; but in order to keep them so, you have to handle them frequently. If you are lifting the hamster out of a box full of bedding or out of a nest, don't just thrust in your hand. First, remove the bedding very carefully; if possible, approach the animal so that it can see you. Now, hold one hand quietly above the animal and close it gently but firmly about the animal, thus cradling its entire body in your closed fist. Never lift a hamster by one of its legs; this might both frighten and injure it. Never lift a hamster from beneath. If it is very young, it will slip from your grasp. If it is an adult, it may bite you.

Handling baby hamsters is an essential part of their care. All young creatures share one vital need—security. A cub should be treated very gently, not be handled too much at the beginning or by too many different people. Often when a baby hamster realizes that it is imprisoned in your fist, it will sob with almost heartbreaking fright. Handle the baby often if you want it to be tame, but do this only for a short while. Then return it to its cage, give it a tidbit, and leave it alone.

Handling Hamsters

Hamsters—especially pregnant and nursing females—sometimes bite, so anyone who handles a hamster should be cautioned accordingly.

Biting

Hamsters bite. For this reason, children should be warned against poking their fingers into the cage. If you tease a caged hamster or handle it badly, it may bite you. Usually the bite is so quick and small that the shock hurts more than the wound. However, an old female—females are more aggressive than males—if teased or provoked, may charge into your hand with such violence and force that she falls backward as she releases it. Such a bite—it is not poisonous—may need the care you would give a cat bite.

Using Containers for Moves

There are occasions when it is more convenient to move hamsters in a container. If you are changing them to another cage for breeding and do not wish to disturb them or if you are cleaning the cage of a mother and her young, you may very well wish to move them by some means other than your hand. A large-mouthed glass jar, a number two and a-half tin can, or a round pound-size rolled oats box provide excellent transportation. Put a handful of oats in the bottom of the receptacle and gently scoop up the

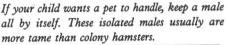

If your child wants a pet to handle, keep a male all by itself. These isolated males usually are more tame than colony hamsters.

Breeding Hamsters

animal you want. While it is busy stuffing the food into its pouches, you can transport the oblivious hamster anywhere.

When you are ready to wean the young, use three-pound rolled oats cartons, one for the males and another for the females. You can then put them in their new cages, to which you have attached the identifying information, thus saving yourself time and energy. Take care that the sides of your container are high enough to prevent the young from scaling them and, so, tumbling out.

Sexing

The female hamster has three external orifices, all lying close together in a straight line. The most anterior is the small, raised urinary papilla. A slight groove leads from this to the vagina to the rear of it. Most posterior is the anus. In fully mature animals, the vagina and anus are surrounded by pigment.

Start handling your young hamsters as soon as possible. In this way they'll be tame.

Breeding Hamsters

The male hamster has two external openings, the penis and the anus. The penis, which is raised and prominent, is located in front of the anus. By weaning time, the distance between the two is clearly seen, a seam or line running between them. As a male hamster nears weaning age, the testes begin to descend and occupy the scrotal sac, giving the male a rounded protruding rear in contrast to that of the female. Hamsters can retract the testes into the body at will and usually do so when picked up, or soon thereafter. As a result, the body outline changes. By giving the animal a firm, gentle squeeze around the middle, the testes will descend into the scrotum.

There are several ways of examining hamsters. If the cage you use has a wired door that swings downward, let the young walk up on it and then swing the door downward. Usually, the males show a swelling that comes to a tapered fullness near the tail. Females are blunt near the tail. If a completely wired cage is available, place some greens on the top. The hamsters will attempt to reach the tempting food; and while they hang upside down, you can scrutinize them. After a while you may be able to identify the males as they walk

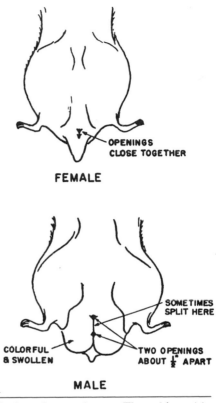

FEMALE — OPENINGS CLOSE TOGETHER

MALE — COLORFUL & SWOLLEN — SOMETIMES SPLIT HERE — TWO OPENINGS ABOUT ¼ APART

Sexing a hamster is easy. The male's testicles are large and prominent.

around the cage. However, the shape of the rear is not always a true guide, for a male non-breeder is often as blunt as a female.

An experienced breeder, who knows what he is looking for, can sex a hamster by putting his entire hand over the animal's body. He then picks it up across the shoulder and lets the body rest supine in the palm of his hand. In this position,

41

Breeding Hamsters

hamsters are generally helpless.

There is still another method of sexing if you are breeding but few hamsters and have them where you can easily see them. When the young are about eight days old and still hairless, coax the mother toward the front of the cage, using some tidbit. Now look at the cubs' bellies. The females will have two rows of dark dots on the sides of the belly—the teats. From the time the fur appears until the young are eighteen days old, sexing may seem particularly difficult; but as they mature, it becomes easier.

Breeding Methods

In livestock production there are three methods of breeding: crossbreeding, line-breeding, and inbreeding. Each of the three types has certain advantages and disadvantages which, if you are seriously interested in improving your hamster herd, you should consider.

Crossbreeding, or outcrossing, means to breed *two varieties* of the same species, which are *unrelated.* An example would be to breed a white strain of an animal species with a black strain, *both entirely unrelated.* The results of such

breeding are the most difficult of the three types to predict, since the interaction of the differing characteristics is unknown. However, it is in just this way, and with this truly experimental type of breeding, that new strains are developed. This method—if you are interested in developing different varieties—is, of course, to be recommended. It cannot be used as a means of fixing characteristics. Mendel's teachings suggest that a crossing of two unrelated well-established strains of hamsters may produce not only an increase in physical vigor but also an increase in undesirable variation, which may appear in future generations. This is the risk of outcrossing. Crossing may endow the offspring with traits which the hamster fancier had no idea existed in either strain.

Line-breeding is breeding along a certain line or direction. It is mating descendants back to a desirable ancestor, as cousin to cousin, uncle to cousin, and so on. By mating more distant relatives, one with another, the danger of degeneration, supposedly attending close inbreeding, is presumably averted. Line-breeding is a type of inbreeding. Following the use of this method, successive improvement may be noted as a

Breeding Hamsters

certain strain of typical size, color, and shape is established. This type of breeding is commonly used to produce show animals.

Inbreeding is intensive line-breeding. It consists of breeding father to daughter, mother to son, or brother to sister. This method of pairing has approximately the same advantages as line-breeding; that is, fixing desirable characteristics of a strain. If the method is used to excess and if the results are not analyzed carefully, the undesirable inherited characteristics may become as strong as the desired ones. Moreover, a general weakening of bodily stamina and degeneration may occur. Many show animals have been produced by this method, which should not be used for any prolonged period.

In 12 days they eat solid food. In 16 days the eyes open; in a month or five weeks they can breed.

Breeding Hamsters

Keeping Breeding Records

It is sound practice to keep complete records on your matings no matter what method of breeding you employ. This does not mean that you should breed only according to the written information you have but also according to your personal observation of the animals.

A good time to begin a pedigree system is when you buy healthy breeding stock ready for its *first* breeding. Designate your females by letter and your males by number. Each breeding female then has a little card tacked to her cage, which holds her life history. In the left top corner appears her letter or a combination of letters. In the right top corner is given her date of birth. Below are six lines representing the six litters (on an average) which a good female is capable of rearing. Record the breeding date or the birth date and the father's number for each group. As soon as you can, fill in the number of males and females in each litter.

At weaning time, the males and the females are separated, each group receiving a temporary card giving its date of birth, the mother's letter, the father's number, and the number of sisters and brothers in the litter. When these animals are mature and put into breeding cages, they receive permanent cards of their own record of reproduction, including litters sired or given birth to and the parents' letter and number.

These individual records, easily maintained, eliminate guesswork and help you to select good breeding stock and cull poor producers. If, for instance, unsatisfactory young are discovered, check the male's number to learn if the same thing happened to other females which this stud served. If so, discard him and use a male who has produced more desirable offspring. Apply a similar procedure to judging the female.

Hamster breeding is still in its infancy. Many mutations are yet to be produced. Since a mutation will be recessive rather than dominant, you should know the breeding history of the mutation hamster. Should you be fortunate enough to produce albino hamsters, a very rare but much-desired occurrence, you can see how vital it is to have a complete and accurate record of all animals involved in that production. Otherwise, all your work might be in vain.

We are now ready to discuss the actual breeding. To begin with, you should breed more females than you

Breeding Hamsters

actually need. This action will compensate for misses, destroyed litters, and an increased demand for your stock.

If you handle your hamsters efficiently, you will not just lump all animals together and then go about your business. Putting a male and female together and then not bothering with them until the next day may result in valuable losses. Furthermore, you are not certain that they have bred. If you are breeding hamsters for your own pleasure, it may not matter which animals breed and which do not; but if you have contracted to supply specific quantities, you must breed systematically, using either pair breeding or colony breeding.

Pair Breeding

When you have chosen a pair to be bred, take the female to the male's pen, probably transferring her in a container. Never bring the male to the female's cage. She is possessive and dislikes intruders.

Be particularly careful when handling a female hamster in the advanced stage of pregnancy. Squeezing the abdomen too tightly can harm the developing embryos, possibly causing a miscarriage or spontaneous abortion.

She will spend every moment of his stay chasing him around, and up and down.

Since the hamster is a nocturnal animal, it will breed more readily at night. If possible, transfer the female to the male then. If there is a little fighting when they are first introduced, it will lead to no harm. Serious fighting, however, should be stopped immediately. Try them again the next night. If the pair is sluggish yet amiable, they may be left together. The chances are they will mate the following night. You must be your own judge in such cases. Occasionally you may plan an important mating, yet the female will not respond. Separate the pair and try every evening until the female will accept the male. This may require as many as five trials. The female is in heat for about twelve hours. In warm climates she

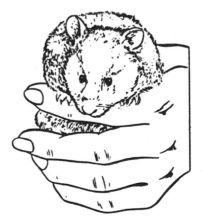

45

Breeding Hamsters

comes into heat once every four, five or six days, and in cold climates, once in five, six, or seven days. If she does not accept the male, take her out after about five minutes. Often females can be tried with that male the same evening until he mates with one which accepts his service.

Bringing an unbred female to a male for her first mating usually presents no difficulty if the animal has been allowed to mature sufficiently and has been well cared for. Unless there is immediate warfare, they will exchange a sniffing of noses and after this brief introduction she will walk off, with her short, stubby tail straight in the air. The male may breed her right

If the female is not ready for breeding, remove her from the male's cage and feed her greens and wheat-germ oil on dry bread.

away, or he may give himself a thorough cleaning first. One type of breeder to beware of is the virgin female who has been slow to mature. If she senses that she is not ready when placed with an older male, she will probably fall on her back and bellow with great sobs. Take her out of the male's cage immediately. Feed her more greens and wheat-germ oil on dry bread. It will be only a few short days before she is ready.

A female or matron that has had young acts differently from a virgin. She may strut about the male's cage as if she were completely unaware of his presence. Occasionally she will rub her rear along the floor to give the male his cue. After she has thoroughly inspected the quarters, she will begin to show keen interest in the buck. They will nibble each other a little here and there, rolling around and scrapping mildly. Soon after, the actual breeding takes place. It usually lasts from fifteen to twenty minutes, and sometimes much longer.

At times, handling a matron may be a problem. On entering the cage she smells the male's nose and then rolls halfway on her side; he follows suit. But then, instead of her tail going up, his does. He has sensed trouble; and in no time at all the

Breeding Hamsters

thought of mating has vanished and there is a rolling ball of fighting hamsters. Just as soon as the female releases the male, he will rush up the nearest wire wall or door; he may attempt even to jump the wall. Every time he approaches her, she charges into him. He then retreats to the corner farthest from the belligerent female and sits there shaking like an old man. Separate the two immediately, else she may ruin him for further breeding. It may take a number of trials before this female is ready to mate, but since matured females give good litters, your efforts will be rewarded.

Here is a time-saving tip. A male's pen that is without food saves much time, particularly with a matron. If the buck's cage is full of attractive food, she will spend her time on arrival filling her pouches to the bursting point. The male may try to attract her or he may concentrate on washing himself. When she has had her fill, she *may* go to him for a breeding; on the other hand, she may charge into him and run about looking for a way out. There is nothing to do in such a case but to return her to her own cage and make sure that his cage is empty the following night.

Colony Breeding

Colony breeding is a common practice used successfully in large

When you place the male and female together for breeding purposes, you should observe them in case a fight starts. You usually can tell by their actions whether breeding will be successful or not.

Breeding Hamsters

hamsteries. Its only drawbacks are that the owner has no way of keeping definite records of individual matings and of correctly estimating the number of young that may be ready for shipping at a future date.

A breeding pen, three to four feet long and about a foot wide, is used for colony breeding. Generally, three males are placed in the pen at one time and in advance of the females. The females are then placed with the males simultaneously. A strange female entering at a later time would be subject to vicious attacks from the others. The animals are left together for from ten to twelve days, at which time each female is placed in an individual cage. The females are checked every two days for signs of swelling. After the twelve-day period, those showing no signs of pregnancy are left in the cage until

they are successfully mated. Even with the female population depleted, no new females should be introduced.

In colony breeding some fighting among the females may be expected. Usually it is not serious. Meanwhile, the males are sleeping in a corner, all curled up together.

Determining When the Female is in Heat

The breeding or heat cycle in the female usually lasts four days, but it may go as long as five or six days. One may say the animal is in heat, or in estrus. In the hamster this

---

You can tell when a female is in heat by examining the exudate which appears in her vagina. Don't waste your time with unripe females since they won't breed but might fight instead.

Breeding Hamsters

cycle may be easily traced by external signs alone. Every fourth morning a white, opaque, mucous discharge appears in the vagina. If the female is lifted by the dorsal skin and turned belly side up, this discharge can be seen protruding from the opening of the vagina. It has a characteristically rounded shape. If the examiner pulls the tail back and downward, or presses gently with the fingers at either side of the vagina, this opaque blob will extend as a rounded viscous mass from the vagina. This excretion is the post-estrous discharge, marking the morning of day two of the cycle. It is the most characteristic and reliable indication of the entire cycle.

The third day may be marked by the presence of a small, leaflike bleb (blister), waxy with definite corrugations. This bleb is not always present; it may be expelled early in the morning and thus be missed. Days four and one of the estrous cycle show no characteristically external signs.

If a female has been checked daily for eight successive mornings and shows the post-estrous discharge on Thursday of the first week and on Monday of the second week, one may be sure that the animal will be in heat again on Thursday night of the second week.

Heat, or the period of sexual receptivity, extends from the evening of day one into the morning of day two (when the post-estrous discharge appears); but fertile matings are limited to the life span of the ova, and the period of fertility is not as long as the period of the female's sexual receptivity. Morning matings on day two result in small litters and a high percentage of false pregnancies. For practical purposes it is best to mate during the evening and night of day one.

If you can devise cages with running wheels which automatically count revolutions, you can tell from the running of the female hamster on which night she is in heat. On this night she may run twice as far as usual. To be more specific, hamsters which regularly run four to eight miles each night show an increase of forty to one hundred percent every fourth or fifth night—an indication of the night of estrus. As a result of the mating, a copulation plug may or may not be formed. This is a large, white waxy plug, which protrudes from the opening of the vagina.

The post-estrous discharge will appear the morning after mating and will blend with the copulation plug when the latter is present. A pregnant female will not display any estrous cycle subsequent to mating.

Breeding Show Animals

Instead, white, translucent moisture will appear at the vaginal orifice, and bits of the plug may continue to be extruded for days. Finally, a copious, waxy substance continues to appear until the litter is born. If the estrous cycle reappears, the female is not pregnant and must be bred again.

Hamsters get their full fur in about two weeks of age, then you can tell what kind of hamsters you raised. It takes just as much work to raise fancy hamsters as normal ones, but you get so much more money when you go to sell them.

In 1945, the British fanciers formed their first hamster club. They aimed to encourage the keeping of Golden Hamsters as pets and to improve them by organizing shows where qualified judges would award prizes to the best exhibits.

At that time, there were no colored hamsters, only varied shades of the ordinary, wild-type Golden Hamster. To help the judges and to ensure uniformity, a written description of the ideal Golden Hamster was agreed upon, in which all the desirable features were listed and a certain number of points was awarded for each feature. This was known as the "Normal Golden Hamster Standard." Later, another standard was drawn up for a darker-colored animal, the "Golden Agouti Hamster," and a third for a light-colored hamster, known as the "Golden Fawn Hamster."

Normal Golden Hamster Standard

Type

The hamster shall be cobby, well-conditioned in body, with large head, broad skull, and short in face; blunt-nosed, avoiding all ratlike appearance. The head shall be well-set in the body, as short-necked as

Breeding Show Animals

possible, with the general outline producing a smooth curve from the nose tip over to nape of the neck. The eyes shall be bold and prominent; ears set well apart, large, and of good width, and carried alert when the animal is actively awake.
—20 points

Color

The top color shall be a rich, deep gold, approaching light chestnut, reaching from nose to tail, free from shading, and of black ticking hairs. Top color carried well down the fur, with a uniform blue-gray undercolor at the base of the hairs. —40 points.

Size

The animal shall be as large as possible, due allowance being made for sex in the mixed classes.
—15 points.

Cheek-flash and Crescents

The black cheek-flash shall be clear and deeply pigmented, tapering to a point ending behind the base of each ear; bordered by the rear white crescent, which shall also be clearly defined and as true white as possible. The front white crescent shall be in the form of a short curve up the face.
—10 points.

Chest Band

The chest band shall be unbroken, well furred, and golden brown in color.
—5 points.

Belly Fur

The belly fur shall be as nearly white as possible, and of good density.
—5 points.

Condition

The fur shall be soft, short, dense, and glossy; the animal well-fleshed and sturdy. —5 points

Penalties for All Standards

Disease of complete intractibility
—Total Disqualification
Wounds, scars, or damaged ears
—Minus 10 points
Dirty staging —Minus 10 points
White hairs on top-coat, face, etc.
—Minus 5 points

Type—"Cobby type" requires the general build of the hamster to be sturdy and thick-set. Sleek, slinky animals are not wanted. The body length should not be more than one and two-thirds times the width across the hips, and the head must

Breeding Show Animals

be large in proportion to the rest of the body.

Head shape is important. The hamster should look more like a miniature bear than a rat. The curve of the head from nose tip to neck should be smooth.

The face should be short and blunt, ears and nose forming an equilateral triangle. The length of the head should not exceed the distance between the ears.

Good type will earn twenty points on the show bench, the standards in this respect being the same for all shades and color varieties.

Color—A common fault is shading, *i.e.*, the color is not uniform but is lighter or darker in places. This condition exists because the brown tips of the hairs do not go down far enough. Below these brown tips the color changes to slate gray; and if this gray comes too near the surface, it will "kill" the top color. The brown coloring at the tips should reach at least one-eighth of an inch into the fur.

Young animals have a number of all-black ticking hairs in their coats; these hairs thin out after about four months, leaving the fur a good, rich gold color. Some hamsters retain these black hairs throughout life, their adult color being more brown than gold. They are the Golden Agoutis.

Long, white guard-hairs occasionally appear on stock, especially along the flanks. Animals showing this fault should not be used for breeding.

Twice as many points are awarded for color as for any other feature. Breeders have, therefore, paid special attention to this feature, and some of the exhibition hamsters seen at British shows really "glow."

Size—Size means a large skeleton well covered with firm flesh. Put your finger and thumb cross the hips of a hamster; then squeeze gently. Bone and meat will hold firm—fat will give. Size does not mean fat. No judge will be fooled by a fat hamster, but he will quickly penalize it.

In some strains of hamsters, females grow larger than males, a condition which is allowed for in the standard. If two animals are equal in *all* respects but sex, the male will be placed higher.

Cheek-flash and Crescents—Crisp head markings on a well-shaped head do more for an exhibition hamster than the ten points allowed. There are three aspects to look for. The black flash should be dark, running to a curved point behind the ear. It should be sharp and clean, not merging into the white or brown nearby. The same applies to the front and rear crescents, which

Breeding Show Animals

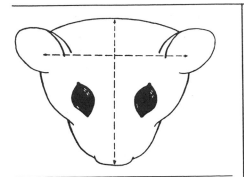

Head shape is important in hamster breeding. Diagramatically, the head should form an equilateral triangle.

should be pure white with clear-cut edges.

Chest Band—The brown dorsal color runs down the shoulders and across the chest underneath. The aim of breeders is to make it join up completely at the chest bone, but very often there is a gap; then the hamster loses five points for "having its waistcoat unbuttoned."

The face markings are important, too.

white crescent   black cheek flash   rear white crescent

Belly Fur—White is wanted, but it is hard to get. Gray, blue, and light-brown colors and thin fur are often seen. This is worth only five points, but British hamsters do not win on top color points now; details count.

Condition—An easy five points! Well-fed hamsters kept in roomy pens will keep themselves in good condition. Careful breeding will give them a running start. Breeding animals must have dense fur. Watch flanks and rump. The coat should be as short as velvet.

Golden Agouti Hamster Standard

Type
  As for Normal.   —20 points

Size
  As for Normal.   —15 points

Condition
  As for Normal.   —5 points

Color
  The top color shall be a rich, dark mahogany red, heavily ticked with black; scalp shading shall be intense, with swarthy face. The undercolor at base shall be dark slate-gray. —40 points.

Cheek-flash and Crescents
  As for Normal, excepting that the

53

black flash shall be more pronounced.
—10 points

Chest Band
The chest band shall be well-furred, as dark as possible, and unbroken.
—5 points

Belly Fur
As for Normal.   —5 points

The standard for the Golden Agouti Hamster is the same as for the Normal Golden Hamster, except for color. The top color is altogether darker and redder, with plenty of black ticking hairs. Young Agoutis have dark, swarthy heads, fading to gray in old age.
This darker shade of hamsters seldom goes to the size of a Normal. It makes them better breeders, for fat causes trouble in the breeding pen.

Golden Fawn Hamster Standard

Type
As for Normal.   —20 points
Size
As for Normal.   —15 points
Condition
As for Normal.   —5 points

Color
The top color shall be a light, fawny gold from nose to tail, free from all shading, and without black ticking or cheek-flashes. Top color carried well down the fur, with pale-gray undercolor at base of hairs.   —40 points

Chest Band
The chest band shall be abbreviated and follow the top color identically, leaving a wide sweep of white center break.   —10 points

Panda hamsters must have panda-like eyes. Jet black, big, bold and prominent.

Breeding Show Animals

Belly Fur

The fur from jaw to anus shall be as dense and white as possible —10 points.

In the Golden Fawn Hamster, no black ticking, and color no darker than nine carat or "Guinea Gold," should be present. Red-eyed animals are disqualified. Since it has proved nearly impossible to close the chest band on this shade, the standard permits an "abbreviation." Reduction in black pigment means almost invisible cheek-flashes.

Golden Agouti and Golden Fawn are *shades,* not colors, and are often put with Normals at shows. Pandas and Creams are judged separately.

Provisional Standards—Pandas and Creams

A provisional standard without point ratings is given for both Pandas and Creams, since at this writing no final standard has been established by any club.

Panda Hamster

The top and belly ground color to be drip-white, without exception, free from shadings or molt patterns. The markings are light to medium tan, as evenly broken and placed as possible; all fur to be very dense, soft, and smooth. The muzzle should be blunt, with a curve-up face. The condition desired is well-fleshed, and as large as possible; the fur soft, dense, and smooth. The eyes to be jet-black, big, bold, and prominent. The ears should be slate-gray, large, well-set, and flawless. The size should be as large as possible, with due allowance for sex. The type is the same as that for Normals.

Cream Hamster

The top color, including the head, should be an even, deep rich (pinky) cream, free from shadings or molt patterns. The belly color needs to be as the top color, apart from the white throat-flash, which should be as white as possible and evenly spaced between the front legs, and as narrow as possible in width. All fur should be very dense, soft, and smooth. The muzzle should be blunt, with a curve-up face. The Cream should be well-fleshed, and as large as possible. The eyes may be jet-black or pink, but should be big, bold, and prominent. The ears to be slate-gray, large, well-set, and flawless. The size should be as large as possible, with due allowance for sex.

Genetics and Breeding

Before giving more attention to practical breeding methods, it is well to have some idea of the underlying genetical principles.

Every physical feature of a sexually reproducing animal like a hamster is determined by a pair of genes. Some features (general size, for example) are controlled by more than one pair of genes. The development of the whole animal is thus controlled by the combined action of hundreds of pairs of these minute genes; and a complete set of gene pairs is duplicated throughout every cell of the animal's body, with the exception of egg- and sperm-cells, in which only one of each pair is present.

Thus, exact replicas of the genes are inherited by offspring *singly*, one of each pair from the mother's egg cell and one of each corresponding pair from the father's sperm cell, only one sperm fusing with only one egg to form one embryo. The two genes, inherited singly, come together in the embryo to form a pair again.

Sometimes two identical genes come together, and it makes no difference which is passed on.

More often, two different genes will come together to make a pair in one parent, and the youngster may inherit one or the other. If one parent has one or both genes in a pair different from one or both genes in the corresponding pair of the other parent, the offspring can inherit two different genes itself. The stronger or dominant gene will then have more influence on the feature for which both genes, as a pair, are responsible. The feature will then be intermediate in quality between the two extremes which either gene would produce unopposed.

Captions

A long-haired satinized dove male hamster, p. 57; a pair of cream long-haired satins, top p. 58; a dark gray satinized angora hamster, bottom p. 58; a normally colored long-haired hamster, top p. 59; a red-eyed cream satinized rex angora hamster, bottom p. 59; a dark gray hamster, top p. 60; a long-haired cinnamon piebald male with two differently colored eyes, bottom p. 60; young females, left to right: tortoiseshell, white-bellied tortoiseshell, light gray tortoiseshell and satinized dominant spot, top p. 61; a cinnamon satinized female and a long-haired cinnamon piebald male mating, bottom p. 61; from right to left: a piebald, a lilac dominant spot, a dark gray satin and a dove, top p. 62; a long-haired satin cinnamon hamster, bottom, p. 62; a light gray angora, top p. 63; a red-eyed cream long-haired, bottom p. 63; a beige hamster, top p. 64; a gray dominant spot and a cinnamon dominant spot, bottom p. 64.

58

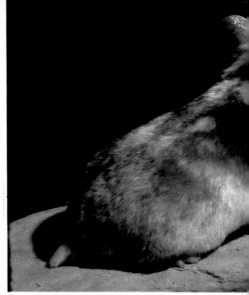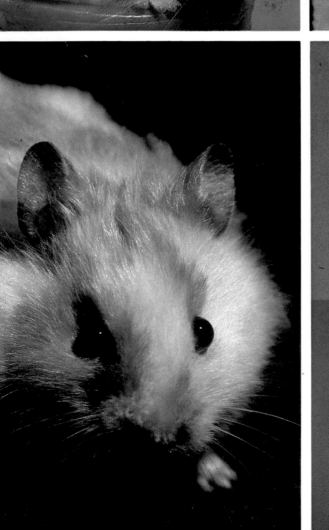

Genetics and Breeding

Sometimes one gene of a pair is so much stronger (dominant) than its partner that the weaker (recessive) gene has no visible effect at all. The gene causing yellow pigment to appear throughout the fur (producing a Cream hamster) is so much weaker than the gene that keeps the yellow pigment in its usual place (as in a Normal hamster) that a Normal by Cream mating produces hybrids all of which appear Normal, although each carries one Cream gene.

If a very weak (recessive) gene is inherited with a less strong partner, it may have more effect. If it should meet a gene identical to itself, it will combine with its partner to produce its full effect. If two of the apparently Normal hybrids previously mentioned are mated together, *some* of the offspring may

inherit the "carried" Cream gene from both parents. The double dose of full-yellow pigment gene will produce Cream Hamsters again, although both parents were (apparently) Normals.

Fixing a Good Feature

Suppose a breeder has one animal which possesses an outstandingly good feature, such as really short, dense fur. If the animal is male, youngsters sired by him may inherit this quality, but *their* progeny may lack it. How can a good feature like this be established so that it will always appear in future generations?

The hamster possessing the desired feature should be mated to one which is as good as possible in all *other* respects. The best youngster from this litter should then be mated back to the short-furred parent.

If *all* the youngsters in this second generation show the desired feature fully, it is likely that the quality is now fixed; but if there is a marked variation in the litter, the best animal should again be mated to the short-furred parent. This entire third generation should show the desired quality of fur as strongly as the original model and should then pass the feature on with little variation.

Some hamsters love the water and bathe continuously, others don't go near the water except to drink.

Genetics and Breeding

Of course, a fault can be established in a strain in the same way. If the original hamster with the fine-fur quality also possessed a fault such as a narrow, snipey head and if the first partner chosen for it also had a narrow head, then the poor head-shape, as well as the good-fur quality, is likely to be fixed. This condition will be made worse if the youngsters selected for mating back also show the head fault. To avoid fixing a fault in this way, do not at any time mate together two animals with the same fault.

Combining Two Good Features

A slightly different problem, requiring a different breeding plan, is posed by the breeder who has a male and a female, each of whom posesses one good feature. The male may have good head-shape but poor color; the female may have good, rich color but a narrow head. How may the two good features be united?

Again, one mating is not enough. If the two animals are paired, their offspring will probably all show only mediocre color and intermediate head-shape. The solution is to select the best pair of youngsters from this first generation and to mate them together, brother to sister. If a second generation of sufficient number is raised, some of the youngsters will show considerable improvement in both features. The remainder will range from good in one quality and mediocre in the other to a few animals that are poor in both features. The latter should be rejected.

A sensible owner will learn as much as possible about hamsters and their care before attempting to breed them.

66

Genetics and Breeding

Correcting a Fault

Fixing a good feature and combining two good features rely upon inbreeding, which is successful only if the very best animals are used and if no outside animals whatsoever are introduced. However a good hamster may look, it will not necessarily pass on its good points to its progeny—it may pass on hidden faults.

However, after some generations of inbreeding and line-breeding, sometimes a fault has been unavoidably fixed in the stock or a desirable feature has been lost. Very often, inbred stock shows a tendency to lose color, with succeeding generations growing paler and paler. Such a fault may pass unnoticed until the stock is compared with some other strain.

If this happens, it will be necessary to cross in a hamster which is faultless on the quality in question. The fault can then be corrected and fixed as described. Before this is done, the newly introduced hamster should be test-mated for any undesirable features which might spoil all the work done on the established strain.

Breeders with ample space and accurate records can avoid crossing in unknown stock by breeding several strains separately. If a feature is "lost" in one strain, it can be "picked up" by mating to an animal in another strain, without having to use an animal of unknown qualities.

General Rules

Start with the best animals available. If possible, your initial breeding stock (or their parents) should between them possess all the desired qualities.

Having started, do not cross in new stock, unless this is unavoidable. Test newly introduced hamsters for faults.

Remember that before becoming visible, faults can be carried and inherited for several generations.

Avoid mating two animals with the same fault.

Watch stamina and fertility. Reject any animal, however good in other respects, which is below standard in these two vital qualities.

Keep records: Name or number every animal, record its parents and its date of birth, and list its good and bad points.

Nest-Building

When you know that your hamsters have mated, you may either remove the female to her cage immediately or let her remain with the male until she shows size—about the tenth or twelfth day. Some breeders who neither wish to colony breed nor have time to supervise the breeding place male and female together and allow them to remain together for at least four days. If you leave the male with the female, see to it that he does not suffer from her aggressiveness.

Preparing the Nesting Cage

On the twelfth day of gestation—four days before birth—take a tall, empty oats box, put new rolled oats in it to occupy the female, and give her cage a final, thorough cleaning. Clean hay, free from dust and pollen, is suitable nesting material, but dried grass is better. Excelsior mixed with newspaper is also recommended. Cloth may be provided, if it is not coarse. The hamster will need enough material to make a nest about six inches in diameter.

The female will need a supply of fresh, clean water. If a drinking bottle is used, it should be placed low enough for the young to reach it as they mature. Very small and shallow drinking pans may be used in place of the water bottle; they must be shallow enough for the young to crawl out should they tumble in. Supply the female with as much variety of food as you can, with the emphasis on protein. A small carrot with top, a potato, an apple, some cabbage, stale bread, a handful of peanuts, bits of cheese, a dog biscuit, nuts, rolled oats, and rabbit pellets—any combination of these is eagerly taken. When you give the cage a final cleaning, provide a large quantity of food to avoid having to open the cage frequently. Although you don't want to disturb the mother any more than necessary, you should keep her supplied with milk. Its use elimates nursing discomfort, which may cause the mother to squeak in pain when the young suckle. A quiet female will jump off the nest and lick the young from her, while a nervous female may not tolerate the pain—and eat the young in frenzy.

Do not handle the mother at all, even if she is your pet. If you must move her, do so in a tall can or carton. Since she is inclined to be restless, examine her wood cage daily for evidence of gnawing. Keep strange persons, as well as dogs and cats, away. Even strange odors may

Nest-Building

alarm a pregnant female or a recent mother.

The New Litter

It will take from a half hour to several hours for a litter to be whelped, depending on its size. While the average number in a litter is eight, it may vary from two to sixteen. The young cubs are born completely naked, covered with a deep-pink, transparent skin; about an inch long, they can crawl when

If your female shows obvious signs of pregnancy when viewed from above, leave her alone as much as possible.

not nested. Their two pin-point teeth enable them through suction to hold to the mother's teat. Only after all young are born do they receive milk. Amazingly, this milk can be seen through the pink chests of the babies.

If a litter is scattered and the young are crawling about, helpless and crying, *leave them alone,* even though they appear to be dead. When the last is born, the female will collect all of them. If she has not been disturbed, she will carry them ever so gently in her mouth and into the nest. If, however, you frighten her or attempt to touch one of the babies, she may kill it or the whole litter.

When the young are seven days old, they are covered with a black guard-coat, except on the belly where their markings when matured will be light. At this time (that is, before the heavy coat has come in) the females are easily identified by the dark dots on either side of the belly.

As the cubs grow older, the tan or golden fur begins to grow. The young start crawling out of the nest—just to have the mother locate them and bring them back again. When they are twelve days old, the mother ceases to clean up their eliminations, and they leave the

Nest-Building

nest—not to be housebroken but to seek food.

Carrot tops should be fed now, together with rolled oats or other grain. Other greens are equally suitable. If you feed pellets and if the only available liquid is the mother's milk, there will be trouble for the young hamsters, since the pellets absorb so much moisture. So be sure to give the young greens, water, or milk. The last mentioned is particularly good for the young. As mentioned, the cage should not be thoroughly cleaned before the young have opened their eyes (fifteen to sixteen days), but clean the soiled corner each week.

Weaning

When hamsters are sixteen days old, they are quite tan; and their eyes have opened. The mother, however, is still in control. Young raised for commercial purposes can be weaned when they are from eighteen to twenty-one days old. Some breeders wean young hamsters when they weigh one ounce (on a postal scale). Future breeding stock should be left with the mother for at least twenty-eight days. Males may be taken away a little sooner.

Hamsters are not suited to serve as foster mothers. They will agree to no arrangement. But when the young are eighteen days old, you can, if you wish, take the males away, replacing them with females of the same age from another litter. This will release one mother for breeding in a short time.

Well-cared-for hamsters mature quickly; in fact, females have been known to breed when twenty-eight days old. However, it is poor policy to start the reproductive cycle then. The litter would probably be very small, and future litters might suffer. You may breed hamsters safely when they are thirty-five days old; but if you wait until they are eight to ten weeks old, your results will be even more satisfactory.

A matron in good health should have three to four days of rest between weanings and breedings. Don't wait too long between breedings, considering, of course, her well-being. The average number of litters a hamster can bear is six, and they should be born while she is still in her prime. Since her life span seldom exceeds 500 days, there is no time for delay. A male will remain a good stud for a similar period, provided he is not injured by fighting females or bred more than four times a week.

Common Ailments and Cures

Hamsters have no known diseases of their own. They are rugged, hardy creatures that can be raised by the thousands with a minimum of trouble, if only you will feed and clean regularly. However, there are a few ailments which you may encounter.

Common Cold

First and foremost is the common cold. A cold can travel through a hamstery as rapidly as distemper through a fox or a mink farm. Therefore, your first precaution is not to handle hamsters while you yourself have a cold; and, second, you should keep visitors from your hamstery as much as possible. If you wish to exhibit a pair or two, separate them from the herd and keep them for showing visitors.

A cold is easily detected. The hamster so affected will not be active; it will sit in its nest with its ears held back against its head. Its nose may appear swollen because the fur is ruffled from a constant wiping of the nasal discharge. If a cold is advanced, you can hear sniffling and sneezing. The animals will lose weight and the coat luster. This condition can be cured effectively if you immediately put the hamster in a clean cage with plenty of warm bedding. Keep the cage draft-free; feed fresh water or milk, stale bread with cod-liver oil, or rolled oats with the oil. The appetite may be low for a few days, but it will soon increase. Do not breed an animal that has a cold. Keep it isolated, and clean and disinfect the cage out of which you take it. Disinfect all watering and feeding dishes. Take care of the sick hamster *after* you have cared for the healthy ones.

Paralysis

Another common ailment is paralysis, which can be avoided in the first place. Give the hamsters cages large enough to permit recreation. A hamster afflicted with cage paralysis will spend most of its time hunched over, often unable to raise its head. Thorough recreation on a table top for about fifteen minutes and then housing in a larger cage may effect a rapid recovery.

Another type of paralysis, more difficult to detect, results from a spinal injury or from lack of vitamin D. The first signs are stiffness of the hands—when the hamster eats, it finds it hard to manipulate all

Common Ailments and Cures

fingers. Very gradually the use of the arms is lost, and slowly death comes. In such a case it is best to destroy the animal.

Falls

All falls do not injure hamsters, but a female in advanced pregnancy if dropped from any height usually dies. This is one reason why pregnant females should not be handled. Usually, unless the falls are especially severe, the hamster is temporarily unconscious; it later revives, as if nothing had happened. Occasionally in such a case a female may suffer a spinal injury which is not apparent, but she will die when she gives birth to her young.

Fly Pests

An insect pest you may find in your hamstery is the *Wohlfahrtia*—a flesh fly hard to distinguish from the common housefly. When this fly is ready to liberate her offspring, she will deposit a mass of living maggots on the young hamsters or near the mother's teats. Even if only one maggot develops, it can rob the mother of much milk. It will grow to half an inch and become quite

dark. It literally digs a hole into the afflicted animal. You can see it occasionally pushing or disappearing in the opening. Be sure you destroy it immediately.

Constipation

Constipation takes the lives of many youngsters between the ages of ten and sixteen days. If you feed the mother pellets, the young may get hold of them as soon as they start eating. Because the young don't get enough moisture, these pellets swell up in their intestines, producing a swollen, discolored stomach and an anus enlarged to three or four times its normal size. Babies suffering from this trouble may be saved, provided the discoloration has not progressed too far up the stomach. Feed juicy greens, lettuce, and apple in a shallow container, with either milk or water. Young suffering from this condition are small for their age; and, unless they have greens, they soon die. As a precaution, feed rolled oats or stale bread when the young first start eating. Pellets as a food are all right, but the babies can't reach the water bottles and the mother probably won't allow them to drink out of a container. If you

The Hamster, A Useful Animal

feed plenty of carrot tops and other green stuff, the mother will carry the green food back to the nest for the young to eat.

Wet tails in adults are attributable to the same cause. The adult hamster seems to waste away, for it will not eat dry food if there is no liquid available.

The hamster's short gestation period, size, gentleness, its reactions

In order for parents and other adults to be able to successfully supervise children's hamster-tending activities, they must themselves know at least the basics of good hamster care.

and susceptibility to human diseases, and its own freedom from diseases—all these factors have made the hamster a preferred research animal. For example, the progress of our knowledge of leprosy had been stopped by the lack of a suitable laboratory animal, but recent reports show that the hamster is susceptible to this terrible disease—a discovery that will materially aid in the standardization of therapy tests to find a cure. Cancer and tuberculosis can be studied effectively by observing their progress in hamsters. Moreover they are contributing to research in polio,

The Hamster, A Useful Animal

spinal meningitis, encephalitis, undulant fever, pneumonia, tetanus, tularemia, and many other disorders, including tooth decay!

The medical and dental professions are, however, not the only ones to whom the hamster is of great value. Fur farmers, snake keepers, and zoos, whose animals require live food, have found hamsters to be excellent. Furthermore, newborn, pre-sight hamsters are pickled and used as bait for game fish. Schools and colleges use hamsters for research and for illustrative purposes in science classes.

The fur of the hamster is lovely—soft, dense, and even-textured. Being uniform and velvety, it responds easily and rapidly to tanning. In the next decade, there may be a greatly increased demand for hamster hides, although now they are not in widespread use.

Hamsters as Pets

We must not overlook the valuable function of hamsters as pets. Because they are small, odorless, gentle, and playful animals, children love them and adults find them entertaining.

Moreover, many people breed and raise hamsters for exhibition, enjoying the challenge of developing improved strains and of "creating" new varieties.

Hamsters are naturally tame; but to keep them so, they must be handled continually. Both males and females may be tamed. Males are always tame after they have become accustomed to handling; females are not quite so friendly during pregnancy and when with new litters. The young should be handled daily from the time they are self-sufficient until they are about three months old. Up to this time they are far too active to be taught any tricks, but they can be accustomed to human contacts. And it is very important that they make a good beginning in this respect.

Taming

Of course, you can also tame older animals. Put the hamster into a cage large enough for it to run away from your hand when you reach inside. If you are using cages with down-swinging doors, you will find it especially easy to handle a shy hamster. Just let it walk up the door; then open the door, letting it swing slowly downward. Now pet

The Hamster, A Useful Animal

the animal gently, using your entire hand. Do this for two or three days every time you feed it. Then let it walk over the back of your hand, gently petting it for a short time with your other hand. These gradual, get-acquainted steps are taken to safeguard the hamster against falls. The animal must learn that your hands don't mean harm, for a frightened hamster may leap from your fingers, fall, and injure himself.

Most hamsters are easily tamed, but wild hamsters are not. There are many hamster farms where hamsters are bred in large quantities. In many cases hamsters get loose and find their way to the nearest barn where they colonize and breed. Leave them alone.

The care given pet hamsters should be the same as that given other hamsters, except that the diet may largely be supplemented with table scraps.

The cage may be equipped with an exercise or running wheel, whether the Ferris-wheel type or the inclined-disk type. The Ferris wheel meets this need better. It should not be fewer than ten inches in diameter, and preferably twelve or fifteen. It need not be wider than four or five inches. The bottom of the wheel should clear the floor by about two inches to prevent the baby hamster from being caught between the revolving wheel and the floor of the cage. The axle for the

The Hamster, A Useful Animal

wheel can be supported by the two sides of the cage; thus, when the wire portion of the cage is lifted, the wheel also is lifted. Most hamsters like to use these wheels, running from four to eight miles a night on them.

Teaching Tricks

The secret of teaching a hamster tricks lies in understanding its spontaneous, habitual reaction and in exercising great patience. For instance, if you put a hamster on the back of your hand and hold it up to a group of people, it will not sit up. Interested in what is going on, it will walk along the edge of your hand, looking down. But this same hamster can be taught to sit up in such a situation. Train it to sit still on your hand; then hold some tidbit over its head for a few times. Soon you will have that hamster getting on your hand and sitting in expectation of something to eat.

Hamsters do not understand words, but whistled sounds may become effective commands. A continual training routine using certain sounds as signals will enable the hamster to establish a habit.

Since this is the only way to teach this animal tricks, you must use much patience.

Hamsters cannot really learn tricks, nor can they react to a human voice like a dog. Their tricks are performed as part of their normal life. Put some games out for them and perhaps they will understand, but it is highly doubtful. At best they react to a whistle if you use the same pitch every time you feed them.

76

The Hamster, A Useful Animal

Raising Hamsters Commercially

Since raising hamsters commercially means the handling of numerous animals, proper and adequate housing facilities are necessary. Without enough cages and with males and females kept in mixed colony cages, you must expect some cannibalism or, at least, some fighting. You might overlook a pregnant female; then, when her litter is whelped, the males and other females would be ready to devour the young as they are born.

Sound equipment for the commercial breeder is the colony cage, with each unit holding *either* males *or* females, and with individual breeding cages to enable him to keep track of all the litters, and so on. With a water bottle and a feeding chute for each colony cage, he can feed many animals in a few minutes. This system also protects customers from accidentally buying bred stock.

It is important to follow a specific feeding and cleaning routine. Feeding hamsters is very inexpensive. Hamsters on a commercial scale may be fed a complete rabbit ration pellet and vegetable trimmings, the latter sometimes obtained free of charge at your local market. It has been estimated that by the time a hamster is thirty days old, it will have cost only eight to ten cents for food. Cages must be cleaned at least once a week to keep the hamsters well.

Besides a feeding and cleaning schedule, you should also have a breeding schedule. Once you know how many animals you can sell, you will find your work very easy, provided that you follow your schedule daily and breed more females than you actually need.

Finding a Market

Where do you find a market for your hamsters? To answer this question, examine your own locality. Here are just a few outlets you should investigate: other breeders, schools, hospitals, laboratories, and research centers. These places are apt to ask for hamsters weighing from fifty to one hundred grams.

Of course, there is a market for hamsters as pets, although the sales are neither so numerous nor so regular as in the institutional field. Should you want to raise just a few off and on, you can take a display cage of these wonderful creatures to the science department of your local school. There the animals will advertise themselves, for the

The Hamster, A Useful Animal

children are bound to find them fascinating. Be sure to have your name and address on the cage so that prospective buyers can locate you. Pet shops and feed stores are excellent outlets for your hamsters as pets; but before you breed your hamsters, check to see if the shop is interested in purchasing stock.

Shipping Hamsters

Let us assume that you have a contact which you are supplying with hamsters and that this contact is located some distance from you. Then shipping the hamsters becomes almost as important as the original raising of sturdy, healthy animals.

The type of shipping container used depends on the number of hamsters to be sent, the material available, and the season. Large numbers of hamsters can be shipped in five-gallon tin cans, but these are undesirable in warm or hot weather. They will hold twenty-four animals if you put in a vertical, middle partition and punch a few air holes (make sure both partitions have these openings). A dozen animals can be placed in each of the two compartments. To fasten the animals in, holes are punched around the open end of the can and a piece of wire is laced over the entire front. A two-gallon tin can will hold a dozen hamsters.

For shipping smaller quantities for breeding purposes and for use in warm weather, wooden boxes are adequate. Wire should be stapled across the top of the wooden box and one side. If you have no lumber

---

It's much better to sell your hamsters to the local petshop but if you must ship them, use a chew-proof and damp-proof container like an empty 5 gallon can with holes punched in it.

The Hamster, A Useful Animal

for crates, use tall tin cans about eight inches high and four to five inches in diameter.

Here are a few don'ts for shipping hamsters: Thin lumber is unsatisfactory, for the animals can gnaw their way through it. Avoid large openings of any kind. Never overcrowd a container. Pellets are inadequate traveling food, because they do not supply liquid. An apple, a potato, or a carrot will satisfy both thirst and hunger. Don't send excellent animals in dirty, rusty tin cans; paint costs but a few cents and dries in minutes.

Have the cans or crates properly labeled and plainly addressed, preferably in two places. If the weather is cold, be sure to put in *enough bedding* for warmth. It is seldom, if ever, wise to ship a bred female; and you should avoid it.

Weight Equivalents

Changing
Ounces to Grams

4½	=	127.6
4	=	113.4
3	=	85.1
2	=	56.7
1	=	28.4
½	=	14.2
¼	=	7.1

Changing
Grams to Ounces

125	=	4.42
100	=	3.53
50	=	1.77
15	=	0.53
10	=	0.35
8	=	0.28
1	=	0.035

Timetable of Hamster Growth

Approximations

Day	Event
1	Birth
7	Black guard-hairs present
12	Leaves nest and eats solid food
15—16	Eyes open
16	Tan color complete
18—21	Wean routine animals for commercial sale
28	Wean Breeding Stock
28	(Females show estrus cycle and can be bred—not recommended)
35	(Males can breed—not recommended)
60	A desirable breeding age

Suggested Reading

YOUR FIRST HAMSTER
Art by E. Videla
ISBN 0-87666-939-9
TFH ST-004

Your First Hamster joins this delightful series of basic pet care instruction manuals that lead readers, young and old, through full-color story panels (there are full-color photographs in Your First Hamster, too) depicting in words and pictures the practical first steps to successful hamster ownership. The large-format 8½ x 11″ book is fun to read and enjoy. It makes a great gift, and it's the perfect beginning book for a new hamster owner.
Hard cover, 8½ x 11″; 32 pages
Full color throughout

TEDDY BEAR HAMSTERS
By Mervin F. Roberts
ISBN 0-87666-776-0
TFH PS-710

Contents: Hamster Facts. Classification And Useful Tables. Hamster Features. You And Your Pet. Choosing A Pet Hamster. Caging. Feeding. Children And Hamsters. Grooming And Bathing. Breeding. Raising Young Hamsters. Genetics. Genetics Glossary. Diseases.
Audience: For breeders and pet keepers a special emphasis on the man-made long-haired hamster variety. The genetics section is entirely new and provides answers and information not otherwise readily available. Grades 8-12.
Hard cover, 5½ x 8″, 96 pages
46 black and white photos, 37 color photos

THE T.F.H. BOOK OF HAMSTERS
By Mervin F. Roberts
ISBN 0-87666-848-1
T.F.H. HP-003
Contents: Hamsters in General. How to Choose a Hamster. Housing. Feeding. Hamster Diseases. Breeding. Standard Features. Raising Young Hamsters. Hints from a Professional. Hamsters in Research.
Audience: Covering every aspect of selecting, housing, breeding and feeding hamsters, this informative volume provides detailed advice for those owning this increasingly popular household pet and is especially valuable for beginners. Disease control and record-keeping are covered in special sections.
Hard cover, 8½ x 11″, 80 pages
89 full-color photos

BREEDING HAMSTERS   KW-134
By Marshall E. Ostrow
ISBN 0-87666-935-6
illustrated with full-color and black and white photos. HARD COVER; 96 pages.

HAMSTERS   KW-015
By Percy Parslow
ISBN 0-87666-923-1
48 full-color photos; 48 black and white photos. HARD COVER; 96 pages.

A rare colored hamster, the dominant spot. Photo by M. Gilroy.